IMAGES
of America

ERIE COUNTY
PENNSYLVANIA

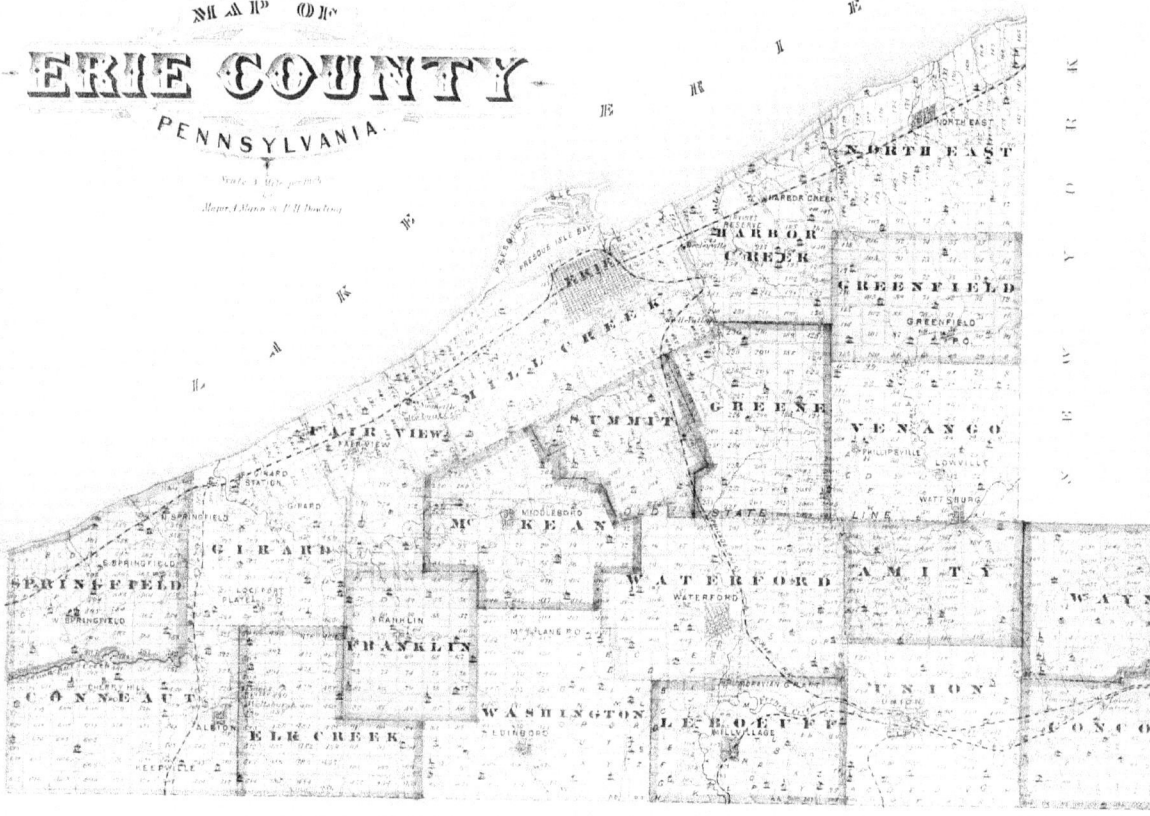

IMAGES
of America

ERIE COUNTY
PENNSYLVANIA

Erie Yesterday

ARCADIA
PUBLISHING

Published by Arcadia Publishing
Charleston, South Carolina

Library of Congress Catalog Card Number: 2007924191

For all general information contact Arcadia Publishing at:
Telephone 843-853-2070
Fax 843-853-0044
E-mail sales@arcadiapublishing.com
For customer service and orders:
Toll-Free 1-888-313-2665

Visit us on the Internet at www.arcadiapublishing.com

Located on the shore of Lake Erie in Springfield Township, this marker indicates the original state line at the 42nd parallel. In 1788 the U.S. government paid Cornplanter and other chiefs of the Six Nations twelve British pounds for the 202, 187 acres in this lakefront triangle. The land was then claimed by five states: Connecticut, Massachusetts, New York, Pennsylvania, and Virginia. In 1792 it was purchased by Pennsylvania to provide access to Lake Erie. The marker was erected in 1906.

Contents

Acknowledgments

We wish to acknowledge the following members of Erie Yesterday who spent many hours searching their archives to supply photos and writing captions to be included in this publication: Corry Area Historical Society, Erie County Historical Society, Fairview Area Historical Society, Firefighters Historical Museum, Fort LeBoeuf Historical Society, GTE Presque Isle Telephone Pioneers Museum, Harborcreek Historical Society, Hornby School Restoration Society, Lake Shore Railway Historical Society, Lawrence Park Historical Society, Museum of Erie General Electric History, North East Historical Society, Wattsburg Area Historical Society, and West County Historical Association.

A special note of appreciation goes to the staff of the Erie County Historical Society, especially the archive section for their invaluable help and patience in helping us find photos and research information for the captions.

Other individuals who supplied material are Lucy Fuller of Albion and Ruthanna Walter of the McCord Library in North East.

Introduction

Erie County lies on a foundation of nearly 7,000 feet of rock layers formed by sedimentation during the millions of years in which the county and the surrounding region were covered by broad inland seas. Beginning about one million years ago, a series of glaciers moved across the area, forever changing the landscape. By 12,000 B.C., the last glacier had receded and left behind the surface features still seen in Erie County, including Lake Erie; the lake plain; the escarpment, or ridge, above the plain; mineral deposits that make up the fertile soils; and the upland topography which comprises most of the county.

Today, the highest ridge is 8 to 10 miles south of Lake Erie. From this point streams flow in opposite directions. The streams along the edge of the lake, such as Elk Creek, Walnut Creek, and Four Mill Creek, cut through layers of glacial drift to form dramatic ravines and gullies. They flow northward into Lake Erie, which eventually flows into the Saint Lawrence River. On the other side of the high ridge, the south-flowing streams are collected primarily into French Creek, which empties into the Allegheny River and on into the Ohio and Mississippi Rivers. French Creek produces a series of valleys with rich alluvial soils suitable for grain and vegetable farming, and the hillsides have a clay loam soil suitable for cattle grazing and dairy farming. Waterpower was vital for running mills and for running machinery in Erie's earliest shops and factories. Early settlement and development was concentrated near the streams.

Presque Isle Bay is the best natural harbor on Lake Erie. The sheltering arm of this peninsula makes the bay a safe harbor where boats are protected from the sudden lake storms typical of Lake Erie. The harbor is still very important and is the main reason why the city of Erie is located there.

Native Americans and Europeans came to settle in Erie County for many reasons, primarily the weather, the geography, and the natural resources. The lake plain bordering the southern shore of Lake Erie has a combination of soils and mini-climate because of the nearness of the lake, which makes this area excellent for fruit crops, early maturing vegetables, and nursery stock. This is the best farmland in the country. Well-drained soils in the upland plateau are well suited to late maturing vegetables, and in the valley bottoms, to root crops.

The first permanent settlers arrived in 1795, and settlement proceeded rapidly throughout the county. The largest concentration in 1800 was in Greenfield Township (pop. 360), where land agent Judah Colt settled. Other concentrations were Springfield Township (pop. 259) along Conneaut Creek, and Waterford Township (pop. 426) on the southern end of the Presque Isle Portage. In 1800, Erie County was created with sixteen townships. By the middle of the century, after a series of name changes and the subdivision of several townships, the county's present-day political boundaries were well defined. Exceptions to this were the creation of boroughs throughout the county, the creation of Lawrence Park in 1926, and the expansion of the city of Erie.

In 1805, two roads were opened along the lakeshore. These roads provided better access to the communities of Buffalo and Cleveland. The frequent stage stops necessary to support travel on these roads encouraged the growth of communities in Erie County such as North East, Harborcreek, Fairview, Girard, and East and West Springfield. Most of southeastern Erie County developed more slowly as a self-sufficient agricultural region, with each area having a small market town to meet its needs. Waterford, located on the main north-south trade route, had an advantage until the Erie Extension Canal was built. Wattsburg was an active community during the early part of the nineteenth century because of its location on French Creek. However, as river traffic declined, so did the fortunes of Wattsburg, which also suffered a major fire in 1928 and a flood in 1930. Some communities such as Union City and Elgin benefited when railroads came through.

Manufacturing was not an important part of the economy during the first half of the nineteenth century. Until 1860, the majority of Erie County "manufactures" used natural resources such as agricultural products or lumber to make products for local markets.

From 1844 to 1870, the county made the transition from a local, largely agricultural economy to a national, manufacturing one. Helping to produce this change were improvements in transportation, including the arrival of the Erie Extension Canal and the railroads, the discovery of oil in northwestern Pennsylvania, the growth of the county population and available labor, and the growth of available capital.

Although the city of Erie was the focus of later growth, other areas of the county continued to develop throughout the mid-nineteenth century. The city of Corry grew out of farmland and forests as a result of the oil boom and railroad linkage. Communities along the lakeshore roads, the Erie Extension Canal, and the railroads—such as East Springfield, Fairview, and Girard— also saw increased economic activity.

The earliest streetcars, or trolleys, were pulled by horses and appeared in 1866. Erie had one of the first electric trolley systems in the country, beginning in 1885. Interurbans connected Erie County to Buffalo and points east, Cleveland and points west, and Meadville to the south. Edinboro benefited from the interurban lines. Its lakeside area was developed after World War I. However, as the county's commercial and mercantile activities became more centralized, the city of Erie benefited most from the trolleys.

Resorts and hotels were built along the bay. A road to the "head," or beginning, of the peninsula was built in 1888. In 1891, a trolley line was laid to Massassauga Point at the head. A few years later the trolley company started Waldameer amusement park at the end of the line, enticing people to use the trolley for weekend outings to the park. Automobiles, buses, and trucks eventually changed the modes of transportation, and trolleys were discontinued in 1935.

Agriculture continued to develop throughout Erie County with a concentration of grape vineyards and orchards in the lake plain area, especially around North East. Processing and shipping of fruits and vegetable became an important local industry.

Throughout the second half of the twentieth century, urban areas have experienced an exodus of people to the suburbs. Agricultural land has been subdivided into residential lots. Townships developed primarily after World War II, and their growth was accelerated by better transportation.

Presented here are the common themes and images of early growth and change in the communities of Erie County that surround the city of Erie.

One

West Erie County

East and North Springfield,
West and North Girard, Girard,
Lockport (Platea), Cranesville,
Wellsburg (Lundys Lane), Keepville,
Albion, and Fairview

Main Street in East Springfield on a summer afternoon was charming. On the road can be seen the recently laid tracks (c. 1903) of the Conneaut and Erie Traction Company. The trolley brought a new mode of transportation to the people along the line.

9

Out for a drive in their Maxwell automobile, this couple posed for a picture in front of the Judd R. Miller General Store in East Springfield. Most small communities had at least one general store where residents could purchase most items needed for their daily life.

Here, some of the boys from the Elmwood Home for Needy Boys are out for a ride, about 1910. The home was located in North Springfield. Its counterpart was the Sunnybrook Home for Girls, located in Girard.

Shown here is West Girard in the early 1900s. Peter Wolverton built a gristmill here on Elk Creek in 1814. Other mills, tanneries, a blacksmith shop, a brickyard, a church and cemetery, a stagecoach stop, and a livery stable also were located here. Wolverton built the first bridge here in 1813. Other bridges were built in 1893, 1894, the 1920s, and the 1950s. The gristmill, rebuilt after an 1840s fire, is still standing.

Nason's Mill was in operation for sixty-seven years, beginning in 1846. It was located on Elk Creek in North Girard and was owned much of the time by J.F. Strickland and A.H. Nason. By the time the mill burned down in 1913, it was only one of two mills left in a township that had once been dotted heavily with them.

The North Girard Band was established by William Daggett early in the 1900s. Mr. Daggett was a carpenter and fisherman with a fishing business at the mouth of Elk Creek in the late 1870s. Most small communities had adult concert bands. Some also had marching bands and brass bands. Summer concerts were a treat!

The Garloch Store was located in North Girard, across from the New York Central depot, early in the 1900s. This community has had several official names. Established as Girard Station in 1852, a post office was located here in 1863 and designated as Miles Grove. The names combined to become North Girard in 1906, and the name was changed again in 1954 to the present-day name of Lake City.

12

The Girard Hardware Store was located in the Union Block, on the south side of Main Street West. It was first established in the 1850s as the John Gulliford Hardware Store. James Sherman purchased it in 1906 and operated it for more than fifty years. In this 1920 photo, Mr. Sherman is in the center.

The Conneaut and Erie Trolley operated through Girard along Main Street early in the 1900s while the system was still under construction. At the right is the Civil War monument, which was first designed with a round footing that was acceptable to horse-drawn vehicles. The footing was redesigned to accommodate trolley rails on either side, thus allowing cars to pass on the single line track.

The West Ridge Transportation Company was owned and operated by F.X. Bowman. Taken in 1927, the photograph shows passengers loading at their home terminal in Girard. The bus line serviced the area of northeastern Ohio, Pennsylvania, and western New York until the early 1950s.

"Bank" barns with a dirt ramp to the second floor were common throughout Erie County. One of the largest was located at the Battles Farm in Girard. Built in 1871, the barn featured a stone foundation and an elegant cupola. It was destroyed by fire in 1977. In its early years, it served as a wintering-over facility for circus horses. Here, the cupola of the farmhouse is visible through the trees.

Images such as this one from the Battles Family Collection are not candid shots. The stamp on the back says, "L.D. Johnson, Portrait and Landscape Artist, Girard, PA-Family Reunions and Picnics a Speciality." Mr. Johnson assembled all the elements of the grape-packing process together and managed to get the people to stand still long enough to snap this portrait.

15

The Battles Memorial School was located in Girard on Main Street East. The building was founded by Charlotte Webster Battles, widow of R.S. Battles, local civic and business leader. Dedicated in 1912, it became a memorial to the Battles family. Restoration efforts failed after a disastrous fire in 1994, and the building was razed two years later.

Students in the first classes in the Battles Memorial School posed before the new school building for their photograph. The names of these children are now reminiscent of all the historic families of the community.

Rush S. Battles and his wife, Charlotte Webster Battles, built this house at Walnut Street in Girard in 1861 at the time of their marriage. Their daughter, Charlotte Elizabeth, lived in the house until her death in 1952. This photo shows the house before a second floor was added to the wing. Today it is the Charlotte Elizabeth Battles Memorial Museum at the Battles Museums of Rural Life.

Miss Battles was very proud of her award-winning flower garden. Walking near the garden at the White House are, from left to right: John Simnacher, Georgianna Read, Miss Battles, and Leah Simnacher. The photo was taken in the 1930s.

In the early 1890s, playwright Denman Thompson presented his nationally-known play, *The Old Homestead*, at the Kibler Opera House to benefit the Girard library fund. Thompson, a native of Girard, contributed greatly to his former community with this production. His play continues to be performed annually in Swanzey, New Hampshire, where he retired.

DENMAN THOMPSON,
IN HIS FAMOUS PLAY
"THE OLD HOMESTEAD,"
AT THE
GIRARD OPERA HOUSE,
Thursday, February 27, 1896.

The Wilcox Library, dedicated in 1893, is located on Main Street East. In 1891, with money raised by the community and a bequest from the will of Robert Wilcox, construction began on a new library. R.S. Battles, a member of the library board, moved his banking business from across the street and built a structure of similar architecture to adjoin the library. This photo was taken in the late 1890s.

Said to be the first monument erected in honor of the Civil War dead, this marble shaft, located in the middle of Girard's Main Street, was dedicated on November 1, 1865, with much fanfare and furor. It was a gift of famed circus owner Dan Rice. Since its rededication in 1965, it has been the focal point of many community activities, including Memorial Day and the Dan Rice Days each August.

Dan Rice, America's most famous clown and circus owner of the nineteenth century, was born in New York in 1823 and died in New Jersey in 1900. Between those years, he rose to incredible fame, made and lost three fortunes, and became a circus legend. At the peak of his career in the 1850s, he came to Erie County and Girard, where he purchased land, built a house, and established winter quarters for his circus animals.

The Gudgeonville bridge spans Elk Creek, south of Girard. Folklore says the bridge was named for a mule that died on the bridge after being frightened by circus music being played on a canal boat. The mule evidently had good ears, for the canal was several miles west of this location. The bridge was severely damaged by fire in 1965 and was repaired. It was rebuilt again by Girard Township in 1997.

The Erie Extension Canal entered Erie County south of Albion and continued through Lockport (now Platea), where this photograph shows the construction of one of twenty-eight locks located there. The locks were used to lower canal boats to the level of Lake Erie. The canal opened in 1844 and closed in 1872, with the collapse of the aqueduct over Elk Creek.

Charles Kennedy and his sister, Dora, were ready to serve in their store in Cranesville (c. 1906). Note the groceries are on the shelves to the left and dry goods are on the right. The store has been the community's main trading center since the early 1800s, and has been in the Kennedy family since 1881. In 1997, the fifth generation of the family are the current proprietors.

This view of the Hotel McMasters was taken shortly before the building was razed in 1876. The hotel was located in Cranesville and attracted the weary traveler during the era of the Erie Extension Canal.

Here is an early view of the Stockdale Block, built in 1874 at Wellsburg (now Lundys Lane). The three-story building is now used for apartments. The first floor originally housed a store, the second floor had offices, and the third floor was used as a meeting hall. It was owned at one time by the Knights of Pythias.

The old Canfield Store was located at Keepville in Conneaut Township into the 1920s. Every small community supported at least one general store, where the local residents could not only buy many of their needs, but socialize and catch up on the local news as well.

The Perry (Carmen) Bridge, built by William Sherman about 1870, was one of the better-known covered bridges in the area. It was located at McKee Road on the dividing lines between Springfield and Conneaut Townships. It was destroyed by fire on April 9, 1996, and a committee is currently seeking funding to have it rebuilt.

The Hotel Albion, on the right (with two balconies), was built in 1901. This State Street scene was taken in Albion in 1910 and shows the new flagstone walks and the beautiful shade trees.

North of the yards at Cranesville is this "Y" on the Bessemer and Lake Erie Railroad. The Y takes the Conneaut branch to Conneaut Harbor and the main branch to Erie. In the last few years, the steam train excursion from Buffalo has used the Y to turn the train.

By 1900, the Albion Depot for the Bessemer and Lake Erie Railroad saw twelve passenger trains roll through each day. The railroad also carried iron ore from Conneaut Harbor to North Bessemer and returned with a load of coal.

On December 6, 1949, the Albion Volunteer Firemen could only stand and watch as their meeting hall and all their equipment went up in flames. One truck that had been stored at Rogers Brothers Corporation was saved. The total loss was $40,000. With the help of local citizens, the company rebuilt and re-equipped.

Three Rogers brothers, Charles, Louis, and Hugh, came to Albion in 1904 to establish a structural-steel fabrication business. They began by building bridges, but by 1914, had built their first trailer for their own use. This single axle trailer, called the Model A, was soon in demand, and many were built to haul such things as coal, lumber, feed, animals, pianos, telephone poles, and, in this photo, milk cans.

Since 1914 Rogers Brothers Corporation has built many types of trailers. In World War I, the company built troop carriers. In World War II, the first contract for trailers awarded by the U.S. government went to Rogers Brothers to build tank retrievers. In September 1942, an Army-Navy "E" Flag (for excellence in production) was awarded to the company by Cmdr. Ralph G. Walling, United States Naval Reserve (USNR) of Erie.

The largest trailer built by Rogers Brothers was constructed for the government in April 1945. This top-secret project was a trailer, 18 feet wide and 40 feet long, with sixty-four desert-type tires, in eight rows of eight each. Shown here in the desert near Alamogordo, New Mexico, it is being pulled by three tractors to test site "Trinity." Its 300-ton cargo was a vessel called Jumbo, built to contain the first atomic bomb.

Curlitt Club (Current Literature) members took part in a 1901 Albion Street Fair. The club was founded in 1896 and is still functioning today.

"Old Home Week" festivities in Albion always included a foot race. Just look at those intense faces on the contestants in this 1909 race on Main Street.

Main Street in Fairview Borough was a graceful tree-shaded lane. Each fall in the early part of the 1900s, it was also the scene of the Republican Men's Ox Roast. In 1908, the day was cold and rainy. The hotel, with porches on two levels, is in the background on the left. The large home beyond that had once been the residence of Dr. Francis Temple, grandfather of child actress Shirley Temple.

Mills were the first industry of Fairview Township. Erie County's second sawmill was built here in 1797 and the first gristmill was built the following year. Other mills included a stone cutting mill, sawmills, woolen mills, paper mills, and many gristmills. The last operating mill in the township was the Lohrer Mill on Trout Run, shown here about 1930.

Since it is bounded on the north by Lake Erie, one of Fairview Township's important industries was fishing. For more than thirty years the Johnson brothers carried on the business established by their father in the late 1800s.

The Caughey Carriage Works was a successful business in Fairview Borough until a disastrous 1886 fire totally engulfed it and seventeen other structures on the north and south sides of West Main Street. The fire was caused by a spark from a sawmill that was blown by a high wind into a nearby stable. Damages totaled $75,000. Fortunately, there was no loss of life.

The soil of Fairview Township was rich and the land was coursed by many streams. One of the many successful farms was that of Milton Donor, who came to the area in 1902. Here, Milton and his son, Earl, work with a team of oxen about 1912.

In 1910, Frank Hetz came to Fairview to plant and sell Christmas trees. His idea grew into one of the largest family-owned nursery businesses in the country. Here, his son, Charles, sits atop a load of brush waiting to be delivered. The bell in the upper left was the fire alarm for many years.

Along the Lake Road in Fairview Township was the White Swan Dairy, owned by entrepreneur George Taylor. Many local folks found employment at the dairy and lunch bar that opened in 1927. The milk was pasteurized, although pasteurization was not a requirement at that time. Here, the employees, the manager and his children, several officials, and even two of the cows pose for a photo. Starting in the late 1930s, for about five years the Taylors sponsored a professional summer theater group who performed in a large barn nearby. The dairy closed during the early 1940s.

A familiar landmark in Fairview Borough was this building owned by the IOOF (Independent Order of Odd Fellows), who purchased it in the early 1900s. It housed a general store on the first floor and a widely used meeting place on the second floor. The building was the center of the community until May 1944, when two trucks collided at the intersection and the building was destroyed in flames.

Built in the early 1860s on the site of a stagecoach inn was the Monitor House in Fairview Borough. As it changed hands, it had many names, but no matter the name, boys always found the porch railing a fine place to view the world. The building was razed in 1994.

At one time in the 1800s, four railroad lines shared two depots and two sets of tracks through Fairview Township. Waiting here at the Lake Shore and Southern Michigan Railroad Depot are men in Union Army uniforms. A few years earlier, Abraham Lincoln had traveled through on this line on his inaugural trip to Washington.

The Erie and Conneaut Trolley Company began operating through Fairview on June 14, 1903, and ended service abruptly on September 16, 1922. The trolley brought many wares from Erie to the rural Fairview community, and made travel to distant places much easier, just as the Erie Extension Canal had in the 1800s. Notice the ad on the trolley's waiting station stating it is only 13 miles to Erie's Boston Store.

These students are on the steps of the large Union School, located in Fairview Borough. By 1900, the school housed all the borough students. Outside the borough, twelve one-room schools operated in the township. The Union School was built in 1891 to replace an earlier building that had burned. The first upper-level grading system in Erie County began in this building, and by 1910 all twelve grades were offered.

At the western edge of the borough was the B'nai B'rith Home for Children, which operated from 1912 until about 1950. During the years that Garson Fall was superintendent (1924–1950), he insisted that every child have the opportunity to take music lessons. Here, one of the younger "bands" lines up in front of the boys' dormitory.

34

A rare and exciting event occurred in August 1911 when a plane landed in a field outside Fairview Borough. Two boys who saw the plane and later became pilots were Neil McCray and Jerry Richardson. Neil started the Fairview Airport in 1928, and Jerry worked for him. Famous pilots Wiley Post and Amelia Earhart came to the airport. To the right, Jerry prepares to take two flappers for a ride.

Small airports started up all over Erie County after World War I. A 1937 Works Progress Administration (WPA) paving project gave Port Erie in nearby Millcreek Township prominence over the Fairview Airport. Licensed as the Griswold Landing Field in 1925, it became the Lincoln Beachey Field in 1929, the Port Erie Airport in 1933, and the Erie International Airport in 1950. The original hangar is shown here in the late 1940s.

An annual community celebration in Fairview is the Memorial Day parade to the cemetery. Early in the 1900s schoolchildren sang and carried flowers in the parade to decorate the graves of fallen heroes. Fairview's veterans of the Civil War were always honored guests.

In 1905, Sarah Struchen was renting this old Sturgeon House (constructed c. 1838). In 1797, the Sturgeon brothers had been the first settlers to the borough area. As a result of the nation's bicentennial, interest in the old house grew, and in 1979 the Fairview Area Historical Society purchased it for restoration as a museum, depository, and meeting room. It was listed on the National Register of Historic Places in 1980.

Two

South Central Erie County
Waterford, McKean, and Edinboro

Waterford's famous Eagle Hotel (shown here in 1900) was built in 1826 by Thomas King as a stagecoach stop and livery. It was owned from 1842 to 1853 by Amos Judson, who came to Waterford in 1798. The hotel was destroyed by fire in 1845 but was immediately rebuilt. It has hosted such personages as President Zachary Taylor and many of the big bands of the twentieth century. It was purchased in 1977 by the Ft. LeBoeuf Historical Society, with members continuing the restoration. The hotel is listed on the National Register of Historic Places.

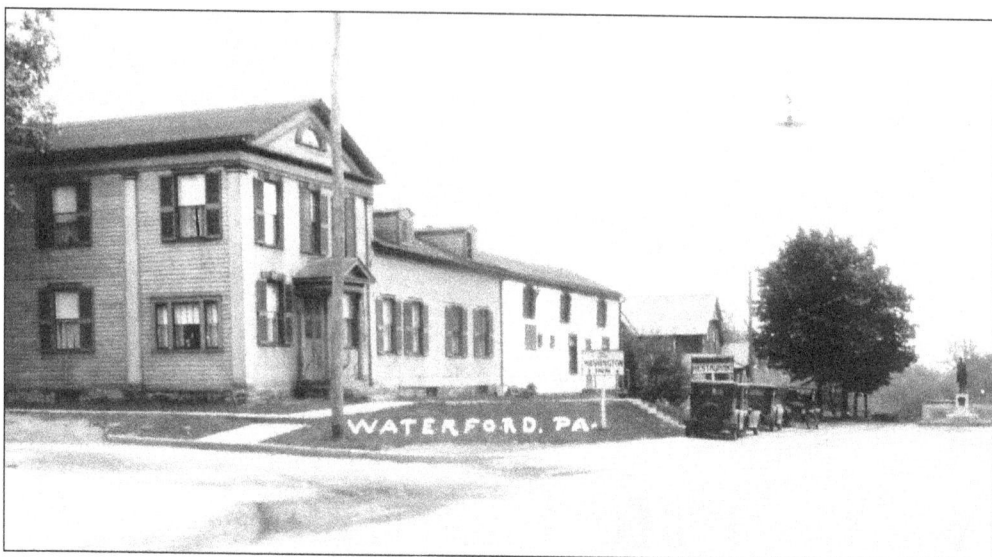

The Amos Judson home was built in two sections about 1820. Judson had come to the area about twenty years earlier. This view in the 1920s also shows the statue of George Washington in its original location in the center of the road. The building is now a house museum owned by the Pennsylvania Historical and Museum Commission and administered by the Ft. LeBoeuf Historical Society.

Here, high tea is served in the Judson House dining room in Waterford, perhaps before 1900. The ladies are Miss Grace Vincent and her sister, Georgia Vincent Berriman, nieces of Amos Judson. Notice the elaborate decor of the house.

An unidentified group of lumbermen posed for this photo on the Knute farm with a clear (meaning no branches) log 5 feet in diameter and 20 feet long. Much virgin timber was cut from Erie County earlier in the nineteenth century, but some tracts survived until the 1890s, as this photo from the Waterford area indicates. Land speculation and lumbering were usually the first order of business on the frontier.

The steam engine accelerated the demise of the virgin forests, as this Waterford area photograph illustrates. Temporary narrow-gauge railroads were often built into the forests to haul away the timber from areas without waterways for floating the logs. Often the bark of trees, like hemlock, was stripped off for use in the tanneries and the rest of the tree was left to rot in the woods.

Chartered in 1811, the Waterford Academy was the oldest academy in the county. It opened in 1826, the same year the Eagle Hotel was built. This 1860 view clearly shows the rail fence, built perhaps not to keep the children in, but to keep roaming hogs and cattle out.

By the 1920s, when this photo was taken of the students at the Waterford Academy, there had been a brick addition and the windows had been changed from nine-over-six panes to the more modern four panes. When the academy was razed, the fan over the doorway was preserved.

40

Mrs. William Vincent, mother of Judge John P. Vincent of Erie and great-grandmother of General Strong Vincent, who was the hero of the Battle of Gettysburg, enjoys some fresh air on the porch of her Waterford home about 1885.

Members of the Women's Relief Corps, which was active in Erie County during the Civil War, posed on the steps of one of the local churches around the turn of the century. The group made quilts, knitted gloves, and provided other supplies to the soldiers, and also offered support to the families of the soldiers. Note the medals pinned on each member of the organization.

Members of the Dr. William Judson family paused in the midst of a Sunday drive about 1890 near Waterford. Evidently the horse found the grass greener just off the beaten path.

Here is a rare 1890s view of a Waterford parade marching south on Walnut Street with the Waterford Cornet Band in the lead. In the background, the spire of the United Presbyterian (now United Methodist) Church rises above the church's horse-barns. The cold Erie County winters demanded that barns be provided for the horses and buggies of church-goers.

Here, afternoon tea is being served on the porch of the Charles and Alice Himrod home at 104 Walnut Street in Waterford about 1910. The residence is known as the Altheim (old country home).

The only known statue of George Washington in British uniform was erected by the Pennsylvania Historical and Museum Commission and dedicated on August 30, 1922, by Gov. William C. Sproul. This photo was taken from the second floor of the Eagle Hotel.

On August 10, 1932, the Daughters of the American Colonists rededicated the site of the 1753 French Fort LeBoeuf in Waterford in honor of George Washington's two hundredth birthday. The south side of the Eagle Hotel is visible to the upper right.

This site of the American blockhouse at Ft. LeBoeuf (Waterford), shown here in 1935, has been preserved by the Daughters of the American Colonists. The blockhouse was built in 1795 as part of the American fort. During the Battle of Lake Erie it was used as quarters for prisoners and the wounded. It was later remodeled and used as a home, then a hotel. It burned in 1868.

A surrey and team prepare to enter the Brotherton covered bridge over French Creek near Juva, just east of Waterford. Transportation on French Creek was an important part of early history in the Waterford area.

Three inland lakes (Lake Pleasant, Lake LeBoeuf, and Edinboro Lake) provided generations of fishermen with recreation and challenge. Here, Waterford residents Fred J. King and Bert Skiff hold up a 32-pound muskellunge taken by Fred on July 8, 1914, in Lake LeBoeuf. A group of unidentified women look on.

Post offices in small communities were often located in general stores. Here, the McKean Post Office is in a store owned and operated by the Leube brothers. Mail delivery by stagecoach began about 1852 and ended in 1900, with the coming of the trolley. The photo is from 1894.

Dr. E.B. Potter's office was in this McKean Drug Store building in 1894. Often a doctor operated a drugstore near his practice in order to dispense medications. Some drugstores were owned and operated by individuals who had little or no formal training. It was not until 1931 that druggists were required to be licensed.

Edinboro incorporated in 1840 on 500 acres of land by Conneautee Lake. An early hotel along the main street was the Robinson House, shown here on the left. It was built in 1843 and razed in 1975. The photo was taken in 1906. Notice the oxen pulling a wagon-load of stalks.

The third gristmill in Erie County, built in 1801 by William Culbertson, was located in Edinboro. The next year, he added a sawmill. This gristmill replaced the earlier one, and was constructed with black walnut beams in the early 1850s. The structure was later purchased by the Borough and was razed in 1959.

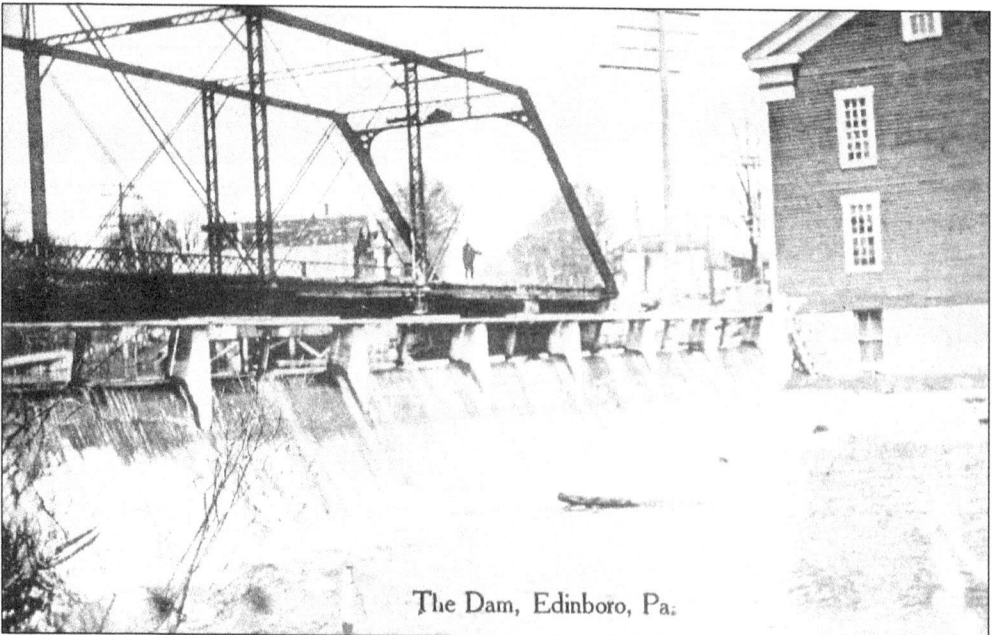

The Dam, Edinboro, Pa.

All early mills were built near streams and powered by water, which required a dam to control the flow. This dam was located near the gristmill shown in the upper photo. Such dams required constant upkeep from weather-related damage.

48

The Erie Plank Road was completed to Edinboro in 1852, passing through McKean en route. A stagecoach line traveled this road carrying both passengers and mail. Here is a view from 1885. Fifteen years later, the stage line was discontinued with the coming of the trolley, which was built along the same route.

The Cutler House and livery were built and owned by H.S. Cutler. The hotel stood on a large lot in the borough, at the corner of Erie and Plum Streets in Edinboro. A public well with an iron pump was located in front of the structure. The building was razed in 1941.

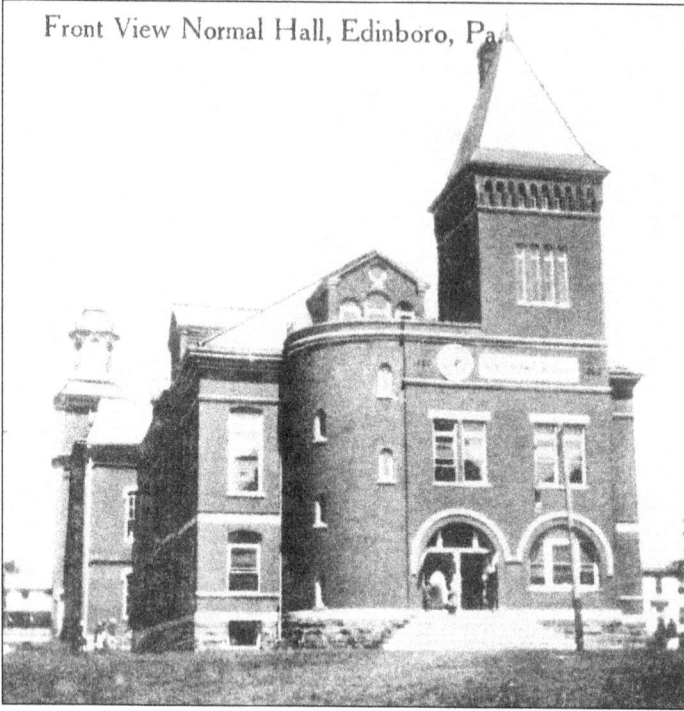

Front View Normal Hall, Edinboro, Pa.

After passage of the Normal School Act of 1857, the Edinboro Academy applied to the state superintendent of schools to provide training for teachers, and this was approved on January 23, 1861. Over the years it has changed with the times, and today Edinboro University of Pennsylvania offers a well-rounded curriculum in many fields of interest for four-year degrees, as well as graduate studies.

The picture, taken right after chapel services, shows the "middle year" spring class of 1911. By this time, the Edinboro Normal School was well established. Many students commuted from surrounding communities by interurban.

Three

East Erie County
Corry, Wattsburg, North East,
Harborcreek, and Lawrence Park

Corry had been a tiny hamlet until 1859, when oil was discovered nearby in Pithole. Four railroad lines rushed to lay track through the area, resulting in a business boom to the small community. By 1866, Corry claimed a population of ten thousand and was incorporated as a city. Over the years Corry has established many traditions. A favorite summer activity in the early part of this century was the Old Home Week celebration. In 1909, the event included this parade.

Hatch School, Corry's first high school, was located on Wright Street, with the first class graduating in 1874. It was used as a high school until a new school was built in 1900. Later it was used as a vocational-technical school and cafeteria. The building was razed in the 1970s.

Old Corry Hospital was started in 1894 and also included a nursing school. Classes were held until 1930. The hospital was in service until 1951, when a new building was erected. The old building was used as a furniture store and was torn down about 1970.

Corry had several floods over the years, and this one in 1904 was one of the worst. The view is of the old Corry Depot on Center Street, looking south.

Some of the snowstorms in the Corry area were so severe that even the streetcar could not get through the snow. In 1916, as many as twenty or more men came to shovel snow so that the car could proceed. The streetcar operated from Corry to Columbus from 1906 to 1923.

This three-story Corry Administration Building was erected on South Center Street in the 1880s. In 1918, the building was destroyed by fire. The building housed the jail in the basement, and one of the prisoners died in the disaster. The fire was found to be the result of arson, and had been set by a fireman.

A large post office building was constructed for Corry to accommodate the great volume of mail processed daily, principally for the Nu-Bone Corset Company. The company sent out about seven hundred packages daily. The post office building was dedicated in 1915.

Located on Route 6 west of Corry, the fish hatchery is the oldest one in Pennsylvania. Originally started as a private hatchery by Seth Weeks in 1873, it was purchased in 1876 by the state and now is operated by the Pennsylvania Fish and Game Commission.

Hotel Corry was built in 1924. Known as one of the finest to be found, it flourished as both a hotel and restaurant. In the 1970s, the name was changed to the Corrian Hotel. It closed in 1991, and the structure is now a branch of Mercyhurst College.

The Climax Manufacturing Company made its first locomotive in 1888 and continued in operation for more than forty years, shipping locomotives to all parts of the world. This Class B locomotive seen outside the Climax plant had eight gears. On display at the Corry Museum is a 30-ton Class B locomotive. Built in 1928, it was among the last to be manufactured at the Corry Plant.

Corry's Aero Supply Company was established in 1913 as Standard Turnbuckle. During World War II, the company employed over 3,100 people, manufacturing turnbuckles and aircraft parts. It was stated that every allied airplane that flew contained a part made in Corry. In the 1960s, the company was purchased by a conglomerate and it continued in operation until 1970.

Sulky racing was a popular activity at the Corry Race Track, as is evident in this 1920s photo. The race track was closed in the early 1930s. A sulky is on display at the Corry Museum.

Corry Fair

This Strobel Air Ship, operated by Jack Dallas of Toledo, Ohio, was an exciting attraction at the Corry Fair. The fair was a popular event for many years and was noted for the wide variety of events each year.

Inez Lord Mecusker was born in 1855 in nearby Warren County and was sent to New York City alone at a very early age to study voice. Her career included four seasons with John Philip Sousa's band. Sousa demanded that his women soloists be highly talented, have a good stage presence, and be pleasing to the eye. Following her engagement with Sousa, she gave concerts all over the United States, and at one point owned her own troupe. She was billed as the "American Cantatrice." She retired to Corry, where she died in 1941 at age eighty-five and was buried in Pine Grove Cemetery. Here, at a high point in her career, she performs as "Galatea," a statue that comes to life.

Wattsburg was incorporated as a borough in 1833 and during the stagecoach days became quite a metropolis as one of the important stops between Erie and Jamestown. By 1828, a weekly mail route was established between those two cities, whose carrier passed through Wattsburg, walking the entire distance. This view is of Main Street, c. 1910.

Before the widespread introduction of automobiles, the stagecoach was the most popular mode of transportation between communities. Here, driver Perry Church poses with his wagon, which ran a regular route between Wattsburg and Union City from 1910 to 1920.

In 1822, through the influence of early settler William Miles, a bridge was built over the west branch of French Creek. This was not only the first steel bridge over the creek, but was also the first permanent bridge erected in Erie County. Note the old Wattsburg Hotel (to the left of the bridge), where such luminaries as Buffalo Bill Cody stayed when in town. Note also the creamery on the right.

Though the building no longer stands, the reputation of Wattsburg's Creamery remains. Its existence was due to the richness of the surrounding land, which supported many fine dairy farms. The excellence of the creamery's product was legendary, and Wattsburg butter was rated equal in quality and price to Chautauqua butter (which was considered to be the best in the East) on the New York market.

60

Moved in April 1910, this Wattsburg house is seen as it straddles the road. It was moved from one side to the other, a new foundation was built, and an addition was built on the back side. In the early 1900s, many itinerant photographers roamed Erie County looking for likely subject matter and are credited today with providing interesting glimpses of life at that time.

In the mid-1940s, a destructive flood swept through the borough. This house, belonging to the Morgan family, was primarily used as a summer home, but was one of Wattsburg's finer residences of the day. Legend has it that with waters measuring 3 feet or more coursing through town, men pulled on their hip boots in order to carry patrons into the local saloon.

This 1928 fire was one of the greatest tragedies to befall Wattsburg. It started with a neglected cooking pot. The fire, which began on the east side of Main Street, quickly spread along the entire block. Damages were reported at $100,000, but no lives were lost. There were reports that firefighters almost drained French Creek in their attempts to douse the flames.

Stores, inns, physicians' offices, mills, even an opera house—Wattsburg at one time had all the amenities one could want in a community. C.E. Ryan, pictured here with two other men in front of his establishment in this c. 1920 photo, operated one of the first automotive garages in town.

The area around Wattsburg was known for its excellent fishing, and the streams abounded in black and yellow bass, trout, and muskellunge. French Creek afforded superior boating and fishing, and offered ideal places for camping parties such as the one taking place here.

For more than a century, one of the largest and most popular events in Wattsburg Borough has been the annual Erie County Wattsburg Fair, one of the oldest in the state. In the early 1900s, many villagers traveled to the fair via this steamboat. The trip up French Creek from town to the fairgrounds—which was a distance of less than a mile—cost each passenger 5¢.

At the fairgrounds, crowds were huge, like they are in this scene from 1912. Once there, people enjoyed a number of attractions, exhibits, and events, including concerts, speeches, harness races, games of chance, an impressive parade called the Grand Cavalcade, and plenty of food.

64

These are the fourteen members of the Wattsburg Arbuckle Band, c. 1910. Little is known about this organization, including the years it was in operation. It appears to have been open to anyone who could toot a horn, and its members performed in concerts and parades throughout the area.

Of great interest to the children in Wattsburg was the opening of the borough's first soda fountain in 1912. Unfortunately, this establishment is no more.

The borough of North East was ill-prepared to fight the fire that consumed much of the south side of West Main Street (shown here looking west) and both sides of South Lake Street on August 13, 1884. Twenty-one businesses, the Presbyterian church, and two private dwellings were leveled. Borough officials took immediate action to establish a 10-mile water system that included downtown hydrants. Three-story buildings were no longer permitted to be constructed. The three-story buildings that remain on East Main Street were missed by the fire. Two volunteer hose companies were soon organized after the fire.

South Lake Street intersects with North East's Main Street. In 1909, this busy street in the downtown area listed such stores as a barber shop, hardware store, a jeweler, books and stationery, furniture, a bank, two newspapers, an optician, two doctors' offices, a plumbing business, a photographer, restaurant, a dry goods store, and more.

The Brawley House was built in North East in 1831 by William Lucius Hall, who later sold it to R.S. Brawley. In 1906, a twenty-five cent "square meal" served there consisted of meat, potatoes, pickles, bread, butter, tea, and coffee. Dessert was extra, but the house offered "music while you eat." The building was torn down in 1913 to make way for the McCord Memorial Library.

The Lake Shore Seminary for Boys and Girls was built in 1871 and prospered until 1878. Three years later, the building was purchased by the Redemptorist Fathers of Pennsylvania for the Catholic Diocese of Erie, and St. Mary's Seminary for aspiring priests was founded. By 1902, the building on the right and the chapel on the left were added. The seminary closed in 1987 for lack of students. Today the building operates as the North East branch of Erie's Mercyhurst College.

This frame structure was the second of the Methodist churches in North East. It was built in 1852, and some of the bricks from the original structure were used in its construction. By 1903, a new church was needed, and the frame church was moved to the back of the lot while a new brick church was being constructed.

Erie County's grape industry began near North East, along the shore of Lake Erie, about 1850. It prospered in the rich soil, with climate tempered by the lake, in the region that was known as the Chautauqua Erie Fruit Belt. For a period of fifteen years the principal use for grapes was to make wine and juices. By the 1870s, grapes were used for table consumption as well. These ladies were harvesting grapes at the turn of the century.

Four generations of Bostwicks have farmed in North East Township. The men in hats are DeWitt Clinton Bostwick (right) and his son, George, who posed with the grape pickers in front of the packing house. The women, who came from North East, Erie, and other communities, roomed on the second floor during the season. The social event of the year was a dance in the borough for all the workers.

Seen here in the spring of the late 1940s, these workers were planting grapevine cuttings. They were taken up in the fall, held in cold storage, and then sold to farmers the following spring. The National Grape Co-op rented the land for this project from the North East Cemetery. Today the area is the "new" part of the cemetery.

Several preserving and canning factories were located along the railroad tracks in North East. Among them were the Fink and McLaughlin Preserving Works. The freight station is located on the extreme left.

70

Women worked alongside men in the grape vineyards around North East. In 1938, Mary Foye Woodhouse drove the tractor on the Foye's farm.

During World War II, this group called themselves the Girls Victory Land Army. They were cherry pickers and lived in cottages nearby. They are seen here in this 1944 photograph, with the drivers (on the right) who took them to the fields. The housekeeper and chaperones are on the left.

The Erie Rapid Transit Trolley approaches North East from the New York state line at Twenty Mile Creek on the Waynehurst trestle and begins its climb up a steep bank. After changes in the route in 1911, this crossing at Twenty Mile Creek became the highest trolley bridge in the world (90 feet high and 900 feet long).

The trolley began operation through North East in 1901 with great fanfare. Within two years the line had been extended to Ripley, New York. Tracks approached the east side of the borough from Mills Woods, on the north side of what is now Route 20. At one time, the line also branched off to popular Orchard Beach.

About 1907, the Buffalo and Lake Erie Traction Company bought the Orchard Beach area along Lake Erie to promote trolley travel. The trolley from North East ran every few minutes, and in the early 1920s, sometimes as many as 647 cars a day made the trip. The "Toboggan" ride down the slide from the bathhouse into the water was a popular feature.

There were other means of getting to Orchard Beach, and one included a bandwagon ride. Here, riding on what is described as a large lifeboat on wheels, this group poses on their way to a fun outing. The area was a popular spot for picnics, reunions, swimming, and dancing.

In 1906, the Fuller Hose Company of North East stood ready to march in the parade to celebrate the Silver Jubilee of St. Mary's Seminary. The two-day celebration included speakers, a Solemn Pontifical Mass, competitions, exhibition drills, and a grand parade. The buildings along the streets were lavishly decorated for the event.

Alfred Short, businessman and civic leader, built a magnificent Victorian mansion in North East in 1887. Sixteen years later, Frank Bowman purchased the dwelling and turned it into a hotel, adding a colonial-type structure on the north end and calling the entire complex the Colonial Hotel. In 1946, a fire gutted nearly all of the original portion. The remainder was renamed the Concord Hotel in 1954.

Gibson Park was established centrally in the borough after a gift of land to the North East community by James Gibson. Over the years, trees were planted, and statuary and a fountain were added. Here, the Camp Fire Girls help gather sap for the Red Cross in March 1918. The park is the focal point of many community activities, including Gibson Days, the Cherry Festival, and the Wine Country Harvest Festival.

Pleasures were simpler fifty or more years ago. The Parent Teacher Association (PTA) produced this "Womanless Wedding" in 1930 at the old high school opposite Gibson Park, giving much amusement to the audience. Prominent community leaders were members of the wedding party. The only woman was Miss Montgomery, who was the director.

Harborcreek was one of the original sixteen townships in the county. Early settlers came from many different areas, selecting lands along the many streams and creeks to make their home. No large community developed here, which enabled the township to retain its rural character. The main street, along Route 20, still resembles this early picture.

In 1946, Mary Brownell Behrend, widow of Ernst Behrend, donated her estate to help establish the Behrend Campus of Pennsylvania State University. The estate included this fine home. Mr. Behrend was the son of the founder of Hammermill Paper Company. The college was founded in 1948, and the campus opened that fall with an enrollment of seventy.

Harborcreek lies along the southern shores of Lake Erie within the Chautauqua Erie Fruit Belt. The soil is rich and fertile in this region, and many settled here to farm. Above, this farm couple displayed their crops for sale at their roadside stand.

Agriculture was a principal activity in the early part of this century in Harborcreek Township. Two generations of a family resided in this farmhouse.

The Joseph Young Moorhead house was built in 1837 of bricks made at his own brickyard on the property, although an older part of the house was constructed in 1810. As one of the oldest homes in Erie County, as well as one of the largest, it is an imposing sight. Located along the Buffalo Road (Route 20) in Harborcreek Township, it was moved back 50 feet using horse-drawn block and tackle when the road was widened in the early 1900s.

Elizabeth Jackson and her daughter, Mildred, residents of Harborcreek, sat for this portrait in 1906. African Americans were part of the development of Erie County from its earliest settlement. The largest such community was in the city of Erie, and many lived in other areas of the county as well.

The Backus House, shown here in 1937, was the home of Timothy Backus, born in 1805 to Joseph and Martha Backus, who were pioneer settlers near the village of Harborcreek. Timothy married Sarah McDowell in 1836 and later served as postmaster at Backus Corners from 1844 to 1848. He moved to this Buffalo Road home in 1877.

The fairgrounds in Harborcreek included a Main Exposition Building (shown here), a half-mile track, a three thousand capacity grandstand, and stables. The first fair in 1916 attracted one hundred thousand people. The expositions were discontinued before World War II, and no buildings remain today.

The Fiddle Inn was originally known as the Harborcreek Half-Way House on the Buffalo Road stage line. It was located there at least by 1854, and perhaps as early as 1838. From the years 1898 to 1944, it was known as Knoll's Hotel and was a popular stopping-off point for officials and passengers of the railroad lines nearby. It is still in operation today as a restaurant.

Looking northwest toward the General Electric Erie Works is an overview of Lawrence Park. Construction of this company town began in 1910, when the General Electric Company (GE) selected Erie for a new factory. GE management planned, financed, and erected the original homes, as well as housing to accommodate growth. Lawrence Park has changed little since its beginning more than eighty years ago.

The first church in Lawrence Park was Christ Lutheran Church, dedicated here in 1914. It was torn down in 1973 and replaced with a modern structure.

By 1913, more than one hundred houses, two commercial buildings, a restaurant/rooming house, and a four-room school had been constructed in Lawrence Park. Some of the street names were Rankine, Silliman, and Smithson.

These eight family apartment houses (row houses) in 1919 were some of the 492 units that had been built to alleviate the housing shortage during World War I. The trees are some of the seven hundred planted by General Electric in those early years.

Two early commercial buildings were erected on Main Street by GE. The buildings met the needs of the community over the years, providing a site for such establishments as the first schoolrooms, church meetings, police headquarters, grocery stores, restaurant, meeting rooms, and more.

One of the busy stores in Lawrence Park in the 1920s was the G.C. Denny Grocery Store on Main Street, shown here with owner G.C. Denny, second from the right.

The Priestley Avenue School was a four-room elementary school built in 1913. Several years later, an addition to the building accommodated classes through the eighth grade. Older children attended school in Erie until the late 1920s or early 1930s, when the first high school was built. The Priestley Avenue School was in use until the Wesleyville-Lawrence Park consolidation in 1965, and the structure was then demolished.

Specially dressed for class are these young girls from the 1929 home-making class at the Lawrence Park School.

The New York Central Railroad Roundhouse was built in Lawrence Park in 1913. The photo displays part of a railroad yard which included a bunkhouse for the crews, as well as a restaurant.

The roller coaster is shown after a 1915 flood caused extensive damage to the Four Mile Creek Amusement Park in Lawrence Park Township. The whole park was later destroyed by fire and never rebuilt, although a bridge at the park site is still used by the Lawrence Park Golf Club.

During World War II, a trailer park was located across from the entrance to the General Electric Erie Works on East Lake Road to provide housing for war workers. This area was later developed with primarily single-family homes.

This Stone House, built by the Crowley family on East Lake Road, is believed to have been on the Underground Railroad circuit. It was one of the few existing buildings in the area when GE built its company town. After deteriorating for a number of years, the Stone House underwent restoration and is being maintained as a private home. The photo is dated 1915.

Four

Themes in Erie County
Firefighting, Locomotive Works, Telephone Company, One-room Schools, and Railroads

This 1830 hand-operated pumper, purchased by Rufus R. Reed, was used until 1848, when it was sold to the volunteer fire department in Waterford. Waterford still owns the apparatus, but it can be seen at the Firefighters Historical Museum, Inc. in Erie.

The first fire station was built at West 5th and Chestnut Streets in Erie in 1873, during the hand-pulled apparatus era. This station was known as the Eagle Hose Company and was used until 1902. Notice the hand-pulled hose cart and fancy uniforms.

Station #2 was built in 1876 on Parade Street, between 11th and 12th Streets. This station had a serious fire in the early 1900s which burned the hay loft and part of the roof. The building closed in 1975. The horses were stabled in the station.

In 1903, a new and larger fire station was built on West 5th and Chestnut Streets, facing east. The old station had faced south. The new station, crew, and apparatus are shown here about 1909. The building became known as Engine Company #4.

Capt. John A. Mayerhoefer built this hose wagon in the early 1900s. It was stationed at Engine House #4. Notice how the harness was hung from the ceiling. The horses were backed in and the harness was lowered and fastened, greatly speeding up the process.

The funeral procession of Fire Chief John J. McMahon passed Fire Station #1 on French Street (now the Pufferbelly Restaurant) on August 22, 1915. McMahon had died two days earlier, after being saved from the rushing waters of the Millcreek flood. He was rescued by Firefighter John J. Donovan of Engine Company #1, who died in the effort. The Erie Fire Department has lost thirteen firefighters in the line of duty.

In 1920, the fire department headquarters was located on the west side of Peach Street between 13th and 14th Streets, which is now the site of Griswold Park. Notice the bulldog mascot on the fender of the truck at the right.

The first motorized aerial ladder, a Hayes model, was used in 1916. It was a 65-foot ladder truck with a gasoline engine that supplied electric current to electric motors on each wheel. The chief's car is a 1916 Ford Coupe. Horses were used to pull the equipment from about 1900 to 1922.

The Watson Paper Mill had a general alarm fire on July 27, 1901. The fire was called in at 11:25 am, and it went to a general alarm shortly afterward. The building was located on East 16th between German and Holland Streets.

At 8 am on February 3, 1913, a fire alarm was struck for the Palace Hardware Building on State Street. A second alarm was struck at 8:10 and a general alarm was struck at 8:15.

On June 3, 1935, an alarm was struck for the Great Lakes Transit Freight House, located at the foot of Holland Street. The first alarm was struck at 6:36 pm and a second was struck two minutes later.

Accidents sometimes happen to fire equipment also. Two firefighters were injured in this accident involving the ladder truck at 23rd and State Streets. Notice the Koehler Beer sign on the building at the left.

Parades were a common site on special days. This chemical wagon and steamer, moving west along South Park Row, were on view as they passed in front of the old Erie Public Library, which was built in 1897.

Here comes the fire chief in this parade along State Street at about 15th Street. Notice the policemen walking along the curb line.

Competition between fire departments was common in the early days. Erie won this c. 1925 competition with the General Electric Fire Department.

"OUR NIGHT."

Erie Fire Department Relief Ass'n
FOURTH ANNUAL BALL,

Friday Evening, November 29th, 1901.

DEMULING'S ORCHESTRA.

Everyone who attended the Fourth Annual Firemen's Ball, held on November 29, 1901, had a fine time!

Captain John A. Mayerhoefer traveled about the city by horse and wagon. The wagon was built especially for him and was housed at Station #9 at West 11th and Poplar Streets. The year was about 1918.

When Station #4 was closed by the City of Erie in 1974, a group of firefighters who were interested in maintaining the building as a museum incorporated. Two years later they opened the building to the public as the Firefighters Historical Museum. It contains more than 1,300 items of antique fire department memorabilia, including photographs, fire apparatus, uniforms, and an 1830 hand-pumper.

The production of the Monitor Top 6.7-cubic-foot refrigerator began at the General Electric Erie Works in 1928. This model was built in 1933. Household appliances and freezers were a major source of employment prior to 1955, when the business was transferred to Appliance Park in Louisville, Kentucky.

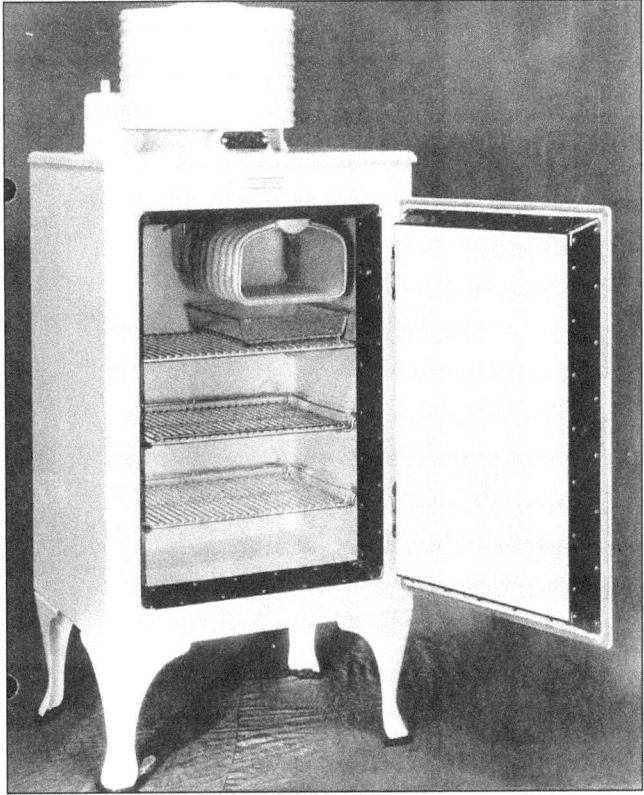

Pictured with a 1937 Ford is a 125-ton, 1,000 horsepower, industrial-type switching locomotive, built the same year as the Ford, with two Cooper-Bessemer engines. The ends of the locomotive were modified to resemble the grill of the automobile.

This type of locomotive, GG1, has been heralded as the most famous electric locomotive in the Western Hemisphere. These locomotives were able to operate at 100 mph. Fifty-seven were built, of which fourteen were assembled at the General Electric Erie Works in 1935. The design was a cooperative effort among the railroad shops, Westinghouse, and General Electric.

In the period when most coal was mined underground, using vertical shafts to deliver miners to the seams and to transport coal to the surface, this low-height, electrically-driven mine locomotive was produced in large numbers. Here, in 1941, one of these locomotives stands before the famous lighted sign at the General Electric Company Erie Works.

Women were employed extensively in both office and plant activities at the General Electric Erie Works. In this 1941 photograph, women are applying insulating tape to coils for use in motors. Motor manufacture was the province of the multi-story Building 6.

On October 8, 1942, a U.S. Army inspection team came to the General Electric Erie Works to study a 45-ton switcher locomotive rated at 380 horsepower. Each end of the locomotive had a complete diesel-engine power plant and controls. These locomotives were produced in great number for use at ordnance plants, steel mills, paper mills, and other industries.

Seen in Building 6 of the General Electric Erie Works in 1944 were some of the 75-millimeter howitzers produced for the U.S. Army during World War II. The howitzers were considered one of the most useful of all army weapons. GE also made a portable power plant for 60-inch diameter searchlights, which were used to spot enemy aircraft. The Erie Works earned eleven government "E" awards for excellence in production.

Above is one of about 1,300 turbines that were produced at the General Electric Erie Works in the World War II effort. A pair of these provided the propulsion for navy ships including destroyers, cruisers, and cargo ships. Buildings 13 and 17 were built specifically to house this assembly operation. This photo was taken in May 1944.

100

Two army tanks were designed at the Erie Works in its World War II effort. One was a 36-ton tank that had a Ford engine and full electrical drive. The other, shown above with the workers who built it, was a 60-ton tank powered by a 900 horsepower Wright Cyclone engine. Only one of this Model T1E1, 60-ton tank was ever produced.

From 1945 to 1949, the General Electric Erie Works produced 111 locomotives for the Fairbanks Morse Company, which the latter would sell and service. Above, two "A"units are coupled and destined for the Kansas City Southern Railroad. The engine had been successfully applied as a submarine engine in World War II.

From 1974 through 1979, the Taiwan Railways purchased a total of ninety-seven electric locomotives for use on their 42-inch tracks. The locomotives came in two configurations—one for freight duty and the other for passenger service. They weighed 200,000 pounds and were 55.9 feet long.

Starting in 1961, locomotives model U25B were marketed and sold within the continental United States to Class I railroads. These four-axle locomotives weighed 132 tons and were rated at 2,500 horsepower. By the 1990s, this GE-developed engine grew to rate 4,400 horsepower. The General Electric Erie Works had grown to be the largest locomotive producer in the world by the 1990s.

From 1876, when Alexander Graham Bell invented the telephone, until 1893, Bell had exclusive rights to provide telephone service. After 1893, when other companies were able to compete, the Mutual Telephone Company was incorporated in Erie. Shown here, from left to right, is William S. Pace of Mutual Telephone; P.H. Adams, who worked on the installation; and John Z. Miller, who became general manager.

A four-position magneto exchange was installed in Erie, capable of serving three hundred telephones. When the exchange opened, it served 170 customers. Local operators handled all the calls. The first exchange was located on the fourth floor of the Trask Building at 9th and State Streets.

At first, the employees were all men who worked at many tasks, including assembling equipment as shown here. Soon women were used as operators during the day and men at night. Business increased rapidly, and a second 400-line switchboard was installed.

Some of the equipment which connected the outside lines to the switchboard is shown here. Local subscribers were able to call any other Mutual subscriber as well as make long distance calls to North East and Girard by 1899 over the lines of the Union Telephone and Telegraph Company.

In 1900, Mutual Telephone erected its own building on East Ninth Street, near State Street. It was equipped with a new multiple switchboard and housed the Union Telephone and Telegraph Company, which offered "nearby" long distance service. This building was enlarged in 1917, and new quarters were built at that location in 1926.

The first general manager of Mutual Telephone was John Z. Miller, shown here in his office with Enith Harris, his secretary.

By 1904, the operators were young women who were hand-picked from the local high school. They not only connected phone calls, but also reported fires, supplied the returns on election night, and obligingly rang subscribers who were concerned they might oversleep.

The equipment room was enlarged, as shown in this 1907 photograph, and operated as a common battery. Customers no longer had to crank their telephones to signal the operator as they did with the older magneto exchange.

The method of constructing telephone lines progressed as did everything else. A horse-drawn wagon and crew performed the task in the late 1800s.

This crew was working hard to hoist the telephone pole in 1905. The poles were erected using manpower, horses, and block and tackle. Notice the ax marks at the bottom of the pole.

Here on 24th Street, between State and Peach, in a later view, the construction crew uses a 1-ton Grabowski truck to work on the lines.

From 1897 to 1926, competition existed between Mutual Telephone and the Bell Company. In order to call all customers who had telephone service, a person had to have a telephone from both companies. In 1926, long distance service was provided over the Union Telephone lines. Here is a sales promotion conducted by Mutual Telephone in 1913.

Mutual Telephone's first overseas call to England on January 29, 1927, represented the first (and farthest west) commercial telephone connection between the United States and Europe. Speaking were John Z. Miller, A.A. Culbertson, and Erie's mayor, Joseph C. Williams. Also present were James Burke, J.J. Mead, James Russell, W.D. Kinney, and J.C. Spencer. Telephone service has gone full circle—from a Bell monopoly, to a period of cooperation between Bell and the "independents," to deregulation of various parts of the industry, to the "breakup" of the Bell System, to competition in the local service part of the industry.

At one time, there were as many as ten one-room schools in Greenfield Township. Hornby School was built and opened in 1875. Its original name was Shadduck School, named for the early settler who built a log structure for his twenty-one children to attend school. By 1956, only six schools remained. With the consolidation of the township, schools were closed and the buildings and contents were sold.

One of the old township schools still standing is the Wildman School, which was named for a local family. It has since been remodeled into a comfortable home. Many prominent local individuals attended these one-room schools and received the very best education available in that era.

The Miller School, named for a prominent local resident, also remains. It was constructed as a two-story building to house the Greenfield High School as well as the local grade school. An addition to the building was acquired by moving the Wilson School House to the site. The high school was in operation until the mid-1920s, and the grade school remained in use until the consolidation in 1956.

Graduation exercises for the last graduating class of eighth graders from the six remaining one-room schools was held at the Little Hope Wesleyan Methodist Church in 1956.

In 1973, as Hornby School approached its one hundredth anniversary, Mrs. Jospehine C. Walter, who had purchased the building in 1956, expressed her desire that the building be restored for posterity.

The first project of the organization was to sponsor and host a reunion picnic honoring former students of Hornby School and of all one-room schools in Greenfield Township. Attending this first annual reunion in 1973 were 225 former students.

Donations from many interested people lead to the restoration of the interior so that it resembled an authentic one-room schoolhouse of the nineteenth century.

The water jug, tin cups, a pot-bellied stove, original school clock, inkwells, textbooks, library books, teachers' souvenirs, various styles of student desks, maps, old report cards, slate blackboards, a teacher's desk, and chair are representative of the items that have been donated and are on display in the School House Museum.

In 1976, the restoration project of Hornby School was designated as the official Bicentennial Project for Greenfield Township.

The Hornby School Museum opened to the public in October 1984. It is used as a living history school museum. Curricula are available for students to visit and experience life as it was in a one-room schoolhouse.

In 1910, the North East station complex of the Lake Shore and Michigan Southern Railway (LS & MSR) included the 1899 brick passenger station (right), water tower, and the wooden freight station (far left).

This wooden structure was built in 1869 by the LS & MSR as a combination passenger and freight station, replacing the original depot, which had been built in 1852. The 1869 building served as the North East freight station until it was closed by New York Central in 1957. The building serves today as part of the Lake Shore Railway Historical Society Museum.

In the early part of this century, travelers relied on interurban electric trolley lines that connected rural communities with larger cities. In this 1912 photograph, a Buffalo and Lake Erie trolley pauses in Moorheadville, along Route 20.

Heisler Locomotive Works in Erie built this 31-ton geared steam locomotive in 1907 for the Smith-McGowin Mill Company of Magazine, Alabama.

Heisler Locomotive Works, located at West 16th and Hickory Streets in Erie, built more than 625 locomotives between 1891 and 1941, when production ended. Best known for its line of gear-driven steam locomotives used in lumbering and mining operations, Heisler also built "fireless" locomotives for industrial applications, as well as a diesel-electric locomotive.

This interior view of the Heisler erecting shop, taken early in the 1900s, shows several geared steam locomotives under construction.

The engineer and company officials of Hammermill Paper Company posed for a picture with their new Heisler fireless steam locomotive. Built in 1939, the 95-ton 0-8-0 locomotive was the largest fireless steam locomotive ever built by Heisler.

"Little Joe," No. 802, was part of an order built by General Electric in Erie in 1947 for the Soviet Union. As government relations deteriorated, the U.S. State Department embargoed the shipment of all strategic material to Russia. The "Little Joe" nickname can be attributed to the locomotive's 89-foot length and the dictator of its intended destination—Josef Stalin. GE later sold the entire order elsewhere, including No. 802, which is now on display at the museum.

118

Locomotives in various stages of completion can be seen in this 1964 view of the assembly floor of Building 10 at General Electric's Erie plant. Building 10 is still used today to produce over six hundred locomotives a year.

Fireless steam locomotives were usually employed in industrial applications where a conventional steam engine could be a fire hazard. This 0-6-0 locomotive was built by Heisler in 1937 for the Cleveland Electric Illuminating Company of Ashtabula, Ohio, and is on display at the Lakeshore Railway Historical Society Museum.

Built in 1915, this fully functioning one-tenth scale model is one of two built by the Heisler Locomotive Works for sales demonstrations of their line of geared locomotives. This model is displayed at the museum.

When passenger levels outgrew the wooden combination station built in 1869, the Lake Shore and Michigan Southern replaced it with this brick and stone structure. Opened in 1899, the last passengers passed through the station in 1960, when the New York Central ended passenger service to North East. Today the building is headquarters of the Lake Shore Railway Historical Society Museum.

Five

The Lake, Presque Isle, and Waldameer Park

Harvesting ice on the bay or the lake was an annual event. When the ice was about 12 inches thick, the snow was scraped off the top and 21-inch squares were marked off for cutting. Conveyor belts, powered by steam engines, moved the blocks from the lakefront to icehouses, where they were stored in layers separated by straw to preserve them for the hot summer days ahead. In the summer, the ice man on a horse-drawn wagon loaded with ice for sale was a welcome sight.

The first lighthouse on the Great Lakes was built on the mainland at Erie, east of Presque Isle, in 1818. Pictured here is the second lighthouse, built on the same site in 1866. The Land Lighthouse has not been lit since Christmas Eve, 1899. When lit, the light was visible for 17 nautical miles. The caretaker's house nearby was built in the mid-1800s.

The lighthouse on Presque Isle was built in 1872 and lit on July 12, 1873. Lighthouse keepers and their families resided in the house year-round until 1939, when it was transferred to the U.S. Coast Guard. The light was automated in 1948 and controlled from the Coast Guard Station nearby. Since then, the house has been rented to civilians, or used as a residence by Coast Guard personnel or officials of Presque Isle.

The USS *Wolverine* lies at anchor in Misery Bay of Presque Isle about 1930. It was launched as the USS *Michigan* in 1844, and was the first iron ship built by the U.S. Navy and the first ironclad on the lakes. The original engines were in operation until 1926. It was the only armed vessel of our navy on the lakes for nearly eighty years. It was scrapped in 1949.

The USS *Brig Niagara* was one of nine ships led into battle on Lake Erie against the British by Commodore Oliver Hazard Perry on September 10, 1813. The Americans were victorious and the surviving ships returned to Erie. The *Niagara*, Perry's flagship, was sunk in Misery Bay to preserve it. Here, the remains of the ship are being raised in 1913 for restoration, to celebrate the centennial of the battle.

These lovely bathing beauties are all dressed up in their bathing suits and ready for a swim. The picture was taken on the beaches of Lake Erie about 1900.

The assistant chief lifeguard on Presque Isle led calisthenics each summer afternoon at 3:00 and 7:00. He swam from Girard to Erie earlier that summer, a distance of 15 miles. The year was about 1930.

The words at the right of these figures say,
"CAST UP BY THE SEA." They were,
in fact, sand art, a popular activity on the
Lake Erie beaches. This scene was created
in August 1913 near Waldameer Park.

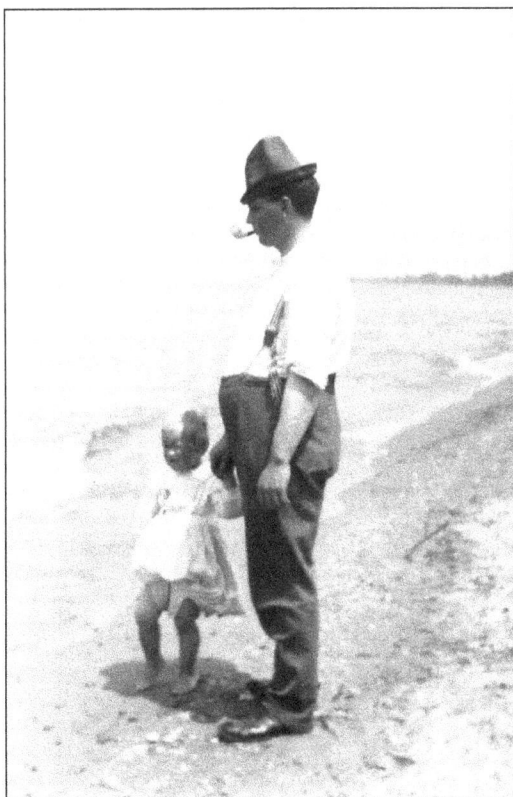

Other popular activities along Lake Erie
were walking the beaches, throwing
"skippy" stones, and picking up driftwood.
Here, Irwin Arbuckle and his child are
enjoying the pleasures of the beach. The
year is about 1902.

Massassauga Point Hotel at "the Head" of the bay, which was the junction of the peninsula (Presque Isle) and the mainland, was a popular place. Erieites traveled the short distance from the public dock by steamer to this popular summer site to dance and attend parties. Built in 1885, it was the second hotel at this site.

Watching the lake was a marvelous way to spend an afternoon, for the view was constantly changing. Here is a scene from the beach at Waldameer Park, about 1905.

The entrance to Waldameer Park, located west of the peninsula, was off West Lake Road, near Wyoming Street. Here is a 1907 view of the main building in this amusement park that also featured dancing. The park remains in full operation today.

Waldameer Park, one of the oldest amusement parks in the United States, opened in 1894. During the early part of this century, the Erie and Conneaut Trolley Company established an end-of-line in that area, which enabled the park to prosper. The wooden roller coaster, called the Figure Eight, was one of the popular rides.

Here's a scene that has been familiar in Erie County for nearly two centuries . . . "Gone fishin'!"

www.ingramcontent.com/pod-product-compliance
Lightning Source LLC
Chambersburg PA
CBHW080856100426
42812CB00007B/2048